MOUNTAIN WILDFLOWERS

for Young Explorers

AN A to Z GUIDE

SHARON LAMAR

2011

MOUNTAIN PRESS PUBLISHING COMPANY

MISSOULA, MONTANA

Dedicated to all children, and to those who are young at heart,
especially Steve, Annie, and Lucas. —SL

Library of Congress Cataloging-in-Publication Data

Lamar, Sharon, 1953–
  Mountain wildflowers for young explorers : an A to Z guide / Sharon Lamar. — 1st ed.
     p. cm.
  ISBN 978-0-87842-578-5 (pbk. : alk. paper)
  1. Wild flowers—West (U.S.)—Identification. 2. Mountain plants—West (U.S.)—Identification. 3. Wild
flowers—West (U.S.)—Pictorial works. 4. Mountain plants—West (U.S.)—Pictorial works. I. Title.
  QK133.L36 2011
  582.130914′3—dc23

                    2011018459

        Printed in Hong Kong by Mantec Production Company

MP Mountain Press
PUBLISHING COMPANY
P.O. Box 2399 • Missoula, MT 59806 • 406-728-1900
800-234-5308 • info@mtnpress.com
www.mountain-press.com

PREFACE

Wildflowers are magnets for children. Little ones are attracted to these jewels of nature. Just like the butterflies, birds, and bees, children cannot resist the bright colors and sweet fragrance of wildflowers. Learning to identify wildflowers helps connect children to nature.

Each year I hike with my first grade students to the Swan River Nature Trail, which is several blocks from the school where I teach in Bigfork, Montana. Here the children learn firsthand to observe the wonderful world of nature. In the natural world, children's senses are continually stimulated. They practice all the classroom skills they have been learning: measuring, counting, calculating, and observing. They take on the role of a scientist in the field by writing and sketching in a journal.

When students are observing and identifying wildflowers, I encourage them to get at eye level with the wildflower without trampling or picking the flower. Almost all wildflowers are fragile and will wilt and wither soon after being picked. We often don't realize it, but wildflowers support entire ecosystems for pollinators, birds, and other small animals. Butterflies, other insects, birds, and animals depend on seeds, nectar, and pollen for their food supply and life-support system. In fact, some pollinators are not very mobile or have small home ranges and die once their habitat is destroyed.

Children have implanted in their hearts a natural love for wildflowers. Anyone who keeps that love of wildflowers in his or her heart keeps in touch with the land of childhood. This book is offered as an expression of gratitude to children for the joy they have brought to my life.

ICONS

The small pictures below appear on each flower page. They are icons representing specific types of information:

 Height: Length of the plant from the top of the plant to the soil level in inches or feet.

 Bloom Season: The time of year the wildflower is in bloom.

 Habitat: The place or environment where the wildflower naturally lives and grows.

 Flower: The part of the plant that produces seeds so new plants can grow.

 Leaves: The (usually) green plant parts attached to the stems. Leaves help make food for the plant.

 Indian Culture Connection: The historic uses of wildflowers among the many Indian tribes in the mountainous regions of western North America.

ABOUT PLANT NAMES

Flowers have descriptive common names that often tell something about the plant: its color or scent, where it is found, what it resembles, or what it is used for. Sometimes the name is the result of a story, myth, or legend.

Throughout history, thousands of descriptive names have been given to plants. It can be confusing when the same plant has been given more than one common name. For example, glacier lily is the common plant name in one location, but it is known as dogtooth violet in another and Easter bells in yet another.

To avoid confusion, a scientific plant-naming system was developed. Plants were grouped according to their structural likenesses. Then each plant was given two names. The scientific system of naming living things is known as the binomial (two-name) system. The two names are in Latin (or Greek), not English. The first name is capitalized and tells you the genus, or what general group a plant or animal belongs to. The second name tells you the species, or the specific name. Genuses belong to larger groups called families, which include plants that are related to each other.

INDIAN CULTURE CONNECTION

For thousands of years, wild plants played a significant role in the lives of Indian people in North America. Not only were plants a source of food, but Native people were masters at using plants as medicine for the sick and injured. In addition, American Indians also used plants as shampoos for their hair, as repellants for unwanted bugs, as remedies for ailing horses, and as spices for their food. Because of their deep respect for life-giving plants, Native people harvested only what was needed so the plants would continue to provide nourishment and healing powers to future generations.

All of the wildflowers listed in this book have a connection to one or more of the many Indian tribes that once inhabited the mountainous regions of the North American West. We owe a debt of gratitude to the Indians who shared their knowledge of the healing qualities of wild plants to help others.

8 to 36 inches

April to July

Prefers dry soil in grasslands, meadows, and open pine forests.

DID YOU KNOW?
Balsamroot is named for the sap in its large, woody root, which smells and feels like balsam fir sap.

Arrowleaf Balsamroot

Balsamorhiza sagittata
SUNFLOWER FAMILY

Arrowleaf balsamroot grows in clumps with a single sunflower-like blossom on each leafless stem.

Each flower head is 2 to 5 inches wide and has 13 to 21 bright yellow ray flowers that resemble petals. These "petals" surround a center button of darker yellow disk flowers.

The large leaves are shaped like arrowheads and can grow up to 12 inches long. Early in the season the leaves are covered with silvery gray hair. Most leaves grow from the base of the plant.

The Kootenai Indians peeled the young flower stems and ate them raw. Some Indians ate the roots. To make them taste better, the roots were baked in a fire pit for at least 3 days. For medicinal use, the roots were boiled and applied to wounds.

6 to 24 inches

June to September

Prefers dry, open places, from valleys to high mountain meadows.

DID YOU KNOW?

Meriwether Lewis collected blanketflower on July 7, 1806. On that day Lewis and nine men crossed the Continental Divide on the return trip to the Great Falls of the Missouri River in present-day Montana.

Blanketflower

Gaillardia aristata
SUNFLOWER FAMILY

Blanketflower has 1 to 3 sunflower-shaped flowers at the top of each stem.

A ring of yellow ray flowers (they look like petals) surrounds the center. Each "petal" has 3 lobes at the tip and tinges of dark red at the base. The central button of brownish disk flowers (tiny flowers) is covered with woolly hair.

The lance-shaped leaves are alternate and mostly grow from the base. The upper leaves vary from toothed to deeply lobed.

American Indians used blanketflower as medicine for intestinal infections and skin disorders, and as an eyewash. The colorful flowers are said to look like the dyed blankets made by some American Indian tribes.

OTHER NAMES

BROWN-EYED SUSAN • INDIAN BLANKETFLOWER

8

8 to 20 inches

June to September

Prefers moist to dry, open or partly shaded forests, grasslands, and mountain slopes at all elevations.

DID YOU KNOW?

The genus name of this flower, Campanula, means "little bell" while the species name, rotundifolia, refers to the round leaves.

Common Harebell

Campanula rotundifolia

BLUEBELL FAMILY

Common harebell usually has several flowers on a long, slender stem.

The purplish blue, bell-shaped flowers, which hang from slender stems, have 5 pointed lobes. The blossom droops, protecting the pollen from rain.

Harebell has 2 kinds of leaves. The alternate stem leaves are narrow, less than ¼ inch wide. The heart-shaped or rounded leaves that grow from the base of the plant wither soon after the flower blooms. A milky juice oozes from broken leaves.

The common harebell was used as medicine by the Cree Indians. The root was chewed to treat heart and lung ailments.

OTHER NAMES

BLUEBELL • BELLFLOWER

10

8 to 28 inches

May to July

Found in grasslands and woodlands of valleys, hills, and mountains, as well as meadows and rocky areas.

DID YOU KNOW?

Meriwether Lewis found wild hyacinth on April 17, 1806, in Oregon. He wrote in his journal: "This hiasinth is a pale blue colour and is a very pretty flower."

Douglas's Wild Hyacinth
Triteleia grandiflora (***Brodiaea douglasii***)
LILY FAMILY

Clusters of bell-shaped flowers grow at the top of each slender, leafless stem of Douglas's wild hyacinth.

The 1-inch flowers are tubular in shape and pale to deep blue in color. The petals are joined together at the base of the flower and flare out about halfway down.

Grasslike leaves grow from the base of the plant.

Some American Indian tribes collected the wild hyacinth bulb. When slow roasted, it has a sweet, nutlike flavor.

OTHER NAMES

LARGE-FLOWER TRITELEIA

12

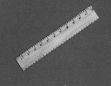

4 to 12 inches

July to August

Prefers moist spots at higher elevations in meadows and along creeks.

DID YOU KNOW?

The genus of this wildflower, Gentiana, was named after King Gentius of Illyria, an ancient country in Europe on the Adriatic Sea. He is often credited with discovering gentian's medicinal properties.

Explorer's Gentian

Gentiana calycosa

GENTIAN FAMILY

Explorer's gentian has slender, erect stems and grows in clusters.

Funnel-shaped flowers 1 to 2 inches long and pale to deep purplish blue grow at the tip of each stem, usually singly but occasionally in clusters of 3. The 5 petal lobes may have dainty greenish spots on the inside of the flower.

The leaves are egg-shaped, $\frac{1}{2}$ to 1 inch long, and arranged opposite each other on the stem.

Native people used the root to make tea and to aid digestion.

OTHER NAMES

MOUNTAIN BOG GENTIAN • MOUNTAIN GENTIAN
RAINIER PLEATED GENTIAN

14

2 to 8 inches

May to June

Prefers shady, moist mountain forests at lower elevations.

DID YOU KNOW?

All orchids are rare and should never be picked or transplanted. Human development has caused a decline of these sensitive flowers.

Fairy Slipper

Calypso bulbosa

ORCHID FAMILY

Fairy slipper is an orchid with 1 delicate flower on a leafless stem. The plant grows from a bulblike underground part of the stem called a corm.

The pink to magenta flower has 5 slender, lance-shaped petals and sepals that look like a crown above a lower pouch shaped like a tiny slipper. The slipper is open at the top and lined inside with purple stripes or spots. It has a tuft of white or yellow hairs on the upper surface.

A single egg-shaped leaf grows from the base of the plant. The leaf develops in autumn and fades the next summer.

Native people used the corms as a food source. They were usually boiled before they were eaten.

OTHER NAMES

CALYPSO ORCHID

16

4 to 16 inches

April to August

Prefers moist soil in shaded to open sites, from valleys to mountain forests.

DID YOU KNOW?

Bears frequently feed on the corms in the spring. The seedpods are grazed by deer, elk, and bighorn sheep.

Glacier Lily

Erythronium grandiflorum

LILY FAMILY

The delicate glacier lily grows from an underground bulblike corm. It blooms as the snow melts in the mountains, sometimes covering entire meadows.

The brilliant yellow (sometimes white) flowers are produced singly or in clusters of 2 or 3. The flower is about 1 to $2\frac{1}{2}$ inches wide, with 6 petals and sepals curving upward from the flower center, while 6 stamens project downward.

The two smooth, shiny, lance-shaped leaves are 4 to 8 inches long, have parallel veins, and emerge from below the soil line.

The glacier lily was an occasional food source for Native people. They ate the bulbs raw or boiled. The leaves were eaten as salad greens.

OTHER NAMES

DOGTOOTH VIOLET • TROUT LILY • SNOW LILY
ADDER'S TONGUE • AVALANCHE LILY • EASTER BELLS

18

6 to 20 inches

June to August

Prefers moist soils in open forests, often in lodgepole pine forests.

DID YOU KNOW?

Arnica species are used in liniments and salves to speed the healing of bruises and reducing swelling. Arnica should not be applied to open wounds.

Heartleaf Arnica

Arnica cordifolia
SUNFLOWER FAMILY

Heartleaf arnica has a sunflower-like blossom on a single stem.

The bright yellow flower heads consist of 9 to 15 ray flowers that are fringed at the tips. The darker yellow disk flowers are clustered in the center of each head. Usually the plant bears 1 flower head 1 to 2½ inches across, but sometimes a pair of flowers arises.

The heart-shaped leaves, coarsely toothed on the edges, grow opposite each other on the stem. The basal leaves grow in clusters.

The Okanagan-Colville Indians used heartleaf arnica roots as a love potion. The roots were dried and mixed with other ingredients to make a face powder.

8 to 20 inches

June to August

Prefers sunny to wooded areas, from valleys to middle elevations in the mountains.

DID YOU KNOW?
Indian paintbrush is a parasite that steals from other plants. A short side root attaches to the roots of a host plant nearby and pulls water and nutrients into the paintbrush's own roots and stems. For this reason, paintbrushes cannot be transplanted or easily grown from seed.

Indian Paintbrush

Castilleja miniata

FIGWORT FAMILY

With its flower spike that looks like a brush dipped in paint, Indian paintbrush is easy to identify.

The Indian paintbrush has a cluster of bright red to orangish red flowers at the top of the stem. The true flowers are actually tiny and mostly green. The intense red comes from the tips of the bracts, modified leaves that resemble flower petals.

The narrow, lance-shaped leaves are alternate and usually 2 to 3 inches long, with smooth edges.

The Chippewa Indians used paintbrush to treat inflammation of joints and muscles. They also used it as a wash to make their hair shiny.

OTHER NAMES

COMMON PAINTBRUSH • SCARLET PAINTBRUSH

22

2 to 12 inches

May to July

Found on moist to dry, open or shaded forests or mountain slopes.

DID YOU KNOW?

Some Jacob's ladder plants smell fine, but others may have a skunky odor.

Jacob's Ladder
Polemonium pulcherrimum
Phlox Family

Jacob's ladder has hairy stems and clusters of eye-catching purple flowers.

The purple to pale blue flowers grow in a cluster at the top of the stem. The 5 petals form a bell-shaped tube with a white or yellow eye in the center and 5 long, white stamens.

The fernlike leaves have many pairs of leaflets, resembling a ladder. Each smooth-edged leaflet is about $1/2$ inch long.

Native people used the plant to make a head and hair wash: all-natural shampoo!

OTHER NAMES
SHOWY JACOB'S LADDER • WESTERN JACOB'S LADDER

1 to 6 inches

April to June

Prefers well-drained, open or wooded sites, from foothills to high mountain areas.

DID YOU KNOW?
Kinnikinnick berries are an important food source for bears. The genus name is from the Greek word arctos, meaning "bear," and staphylos, meaning "a bunch of grapes." The species name is from the Greek uva, meaning "grape," and ursus, meaning "bear." So both names mean "bear grape." In other words, "bearberry bearberry"!

Kinnikinnick

Arctostaphylos uva-ursi

HEATH FAMILY

Kinnikinnick is an evergreen forest ground cover. It has woody, multibranched stems that root and spread along the surface, carpeting forest floors.

Light pink urn-shaped flowers hang in clusters from the tips of branches. Red berries replace the flowers in late summer and remain on the stem all winter.

The shiny evergreen leaves are alternate, oblong, and $\frac{1}{2}$ to 1 inch long, with a leathery texture.

Crow Indians ground the kinnikinnick leaves to form a powder to treat canker sores of the mouth. Cheyenne Indians used kinnikinnick berries in a mixture to treat colds and coughs. Some Indian tribes used the tannin in the leaves for tanning hides.

OTHER NAMES

BEARBERRY

6 to 16 inches

May to July

Prefers moderately dry sites in pine forests.

DID YOU KNOW?

Many lupines have poisonous alkaloids in their seeds. In the Rocky Mountain region more sheep losses have been reported from lupine poisoning than from any other plant.

Lodgepole Lupine

Lupinus parviflorus

PEA FAMILY

Lupine species are easily identified by their divided leaves and long spikes of blue flowers that resemble the blossoms on pea plants.

From 15 to 92 light blue to purple flowers form an elongated cluster on the upper end of the stem. Each banner-shaped flower is ¼ to ½ inch long.

The leaves are alternate and palmately compound, with 5 to 11 lance-shaped leaflets.

Native people were masters at plant identification. They were well aware of the poisonous properties of this plant.

OTHER NAMES

BLUEBONNET • QUAKERBONNET

28

4 to 6 inches

June to August

Prefers moist, open sites at moderate to high elevations.

DID YOU KNOW?

The yellow (or sometimes white) ring in the center of the flower guides insects toward the flower tube in search of nectar. The mountain forget-me-not is the official state flower of Alaska.

Mountain Forget-Me-Not

Myosotis alpestris

BORAGE FAMILY

Mountain forget-me-not is a small plant that grows in low clusters with tiny wheel-shaped flowers.

Bright sky blue flowers with a yellow center grow in clusters on branches. Each flower is less than $1/4$ inch wide, with 5 lobes fused at the base into a short tube. The 5 stamens are hidden inside the tube.

The leaves are alternate, lance-shaped, and narrow, with soft hair.

Native people rubbed this plant species on the hair to act like a hair gel.

OTHER NAMES

WOOD FORGET-ME-NOT • ASIAN FORGET-ME-NOT

12 to 22 inches

May to July

Found in meadows, grasslands, and open mountain forests as well as rockslides.

DID YOU KNOW?

Meriwether Lewis collected this plant on May 6, 1806 in present-day Idaho.

Nine-Leaf Biscuit Root

Lomatium triternatum

Carrot (Parsley) Family

Nine-leaf biscuit root has a narrow, leafless stem topped with a tight cluster of bright yellow flowers.

The tiny yellow flowers occur in umbrella-shaped clusters.

The compound leaves are arranged into 3 sets of 3 leaflets each. The leaf segments are up to 8 inches long and are quite narrow with smooth edges.

Nine-leaf biscuit root was described by Frederick Pursh in a book about Lewis and Clark's plant collections: "The . . . root of this species is one of the grateful vegetables of the Indians: they use it baked or roasted." Some American Indians ate the brown, finger-sized roots. The Okanagan-Colville Indians of the Pacific Northwest used the dried flowers and leaves to season food, giving it a flavor similar to parsley.

OTHER NAMES

NINE-LEAF DESERT PARSLEY • LEWIS'S LOMATIUM

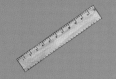

15 to 30 feet

May to July

Prefers dry to moderately moist forests and thickets.

DID YOU KNOW?
The plant was collected by Meriwether Lewis in northern Idaho in 1806. The sweet nectar of the flower attracts hummingbirds and butterflies. Although the opening of the blossom is too small for bumblebees to squeeze in, bees will poke holes in the side of the flower to reach the nectar.

Orange Honeysuckle

Lonicera ciliosa

HONEYSUCKLE FAMILY

Orange honeysuckle is a vine that climbs trees and shrubs to a height of 15 to 30 feet.

The trumpet-shaped orange flowers are 1 to 2 inches long and grow in clusters.

The leaves are opposite and egg-shaped. Just below the flower clusters, the pair of leaves is joined together into a single bractlike leaf and completely encircles the hollow stem. It appears as if the stem passes through the center of the leaf.

The woody vines were used by some American Indians for weaving, binding, and lashing.

OTHER NAMES

TRUMPET HONEYSUCKLE

34

6 to 12 inches

June to July

Prefers coniferous forests, meadows, and grasslands.

DID YOU KNOW?

The name Calochortus comes from the Greek kalos, meaning "beautiful," and chortos, meaning "grass." The name apiculatus means "small-pointed."

Pointed Mariposa Lily

Calochortus apiculatus

LILY FAMILY

Pointed mariposa lily grows from an egg-shaped bulb. The smooth stem supports 1 to 5 white flowers with 2 or 3 leafy bracts near the top.

The flower has 3 white, wedge-shaped petals and 3 narrow green sepals. The petals are hairy on the inner surface and pointed at the tip. A tiny purple dot is near the base of each petal.

A single leaf, shorter than the stem, grows from the base of the plant. The leaf is about ¼ inch wide, tapering to a point.

The bulbs of many species of *Calochortus* were eaten by Native Americans.

OTHER NAMES

BAKER MARIPOSA LILY

THREE-SPOT MARIPOSA • PURPLE-EYED MARIPOSA

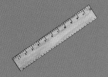

3 to 8 inches

June to July

Prefers moist soils in shaded coniferous forests.

DID YOU KNOW?
The berries have a foul flavor, but grouse seem to enjoy eating them. The genus name Clintonia *was chosen in honor of DeWitt Clinton (1769–1828), a naturalist and governor of New York. The species name* uniflora *is from the Latin word* unus, *meaning "one," and* floris, *meaning "flower": thus, "one-flowered."*

Queen's Cup Beadlily

Clintonia uniflora

LILY FAMILY

With its petals and sepals the same size, the symmetrical queen's cup beadlily looks like royalty. Woolly hair grows on the leaves, stem, petals, and stamens.

A single white flower grows at the top of the stem. The 3 white petals and 3 sepals spread outward in the shape of a star, revealing 6 yellow stamens. Later in the season the flower is replaced by a single beadlike, metallic blue berry.

The 2 or 3 leaves grow from the base and are usually longer than the stem. They are bright green and oval-shaped, with parallel veins.

The corms of the plant were eaten raw or cooked by Native Americans.

OTHER NAMES
BRIDE'S BONNET

38

3 to 6 feet

May to July

Found in moist areas along hillsides and banks of streams and ponds.

DID YOU KNOW?
Rose hips are high in vitamins A and C. Rose hip tea is popular and is sometimes drunk to guard against colds and flu.

Rose (Wild)

Rosa woodsii
ROSE FAMILY

Wild rose is a branched shrub with prickly or bristly stems and pink flowers.

The fragrant pink flower grows singly or in clusters and has 5 petals, 5 green sepals, and numerous stamens. The round, red, berrylike fruits, called rose hips, stay on the plant during winter.

The compound leaves have 3 to 9 leaflets with toothed edges. Two sharp thorns are located at the base of each leaf.

Cheyenne, Kootenai, Gros Ventre, Blackfeet, and Crow Indians brewed tea from the stem or root bark. Crow Indians crushed and seeded the rose hips before mixing them with tallow to store for winter use.

OTHER NAMES
WOODS ROSE

6 to 12 inches

April to August

Prefers moist mountain meadows and stream banks, from valleys to mountains.

DID YOU KNOW?
Pollination is aided by "buzz pollination," when the rapid buzzing of a bee vibrates the stamen, causing the pollen to discharge.

Shooting Star
Dodecatheon pulchellum
PRIMROSE FAMILY

Shooting star has a leafless stem with bright pink flowers that look like small rockets.

The 5 pink to magenta petals bend backward from a yellow base to reveal 5 fused stamens like the tip of a rocket pointing downward.

The lance-shaped to spoon-shaped leaves grow from the base of the plant and surround the stem.

An infusion of the roots was used as a wash for sore eyes by the Blackfeet and Okanagan-Colville Indians.

OTHER NAMES
FEW-FLOWERED SHOOTING STAR
PRETTY SHOOTING STAR • WOODLAND SHOOTING STAR

42

4 to 16 inches

March to June

Prefers wet, shady sites in coniferous forests.

DID YOU KNOW?

The word trillium comes from the Latin word tri, meaning "three," referring to the plant's leaves, petals, sepals, and stigmas, which all occur in sets of 3.

Trillium

Trillium ovatum
Lily Family

One of the first flowers to bloom in the spring, trillium has distinctive white 3-petaled blossoms.

The single flower has 3 white petals, 3 green sepals, and 6 yellow stamens. Amazingly, as the flower ages the petals turn from white to pink or lavender!

A set of 3 leaves grows at the top of the stem, just below the flower. Each oval leaf is 1 to 5 inches long, with a pointed tip.

Some Native American tribes used trillium for pain during childbirth, which is where the name birth-root comes from.

OTHER NAMES

WAKE ROBIN • BIRTH-ROOT

44

2 to 6 feet

May to July

Prefers moist soil in open coniferous forests.

Utah Honeysuckle

Lonicera utahensis

HONEYSUCKLE FAMILY

Utah honeysuckle is a forest shrub with branched, leafy stems.

The creamy white, tube-shaped flowers are arranged in pairs growing from the joint between the leaf and stem. A small bulge extends from the base of each flower. As the season progresses, the flowers are replaced by red twin berries.

The opposite leaves are egg-shaped and rounded on the ends.

Okanagan-Colville Indians steeped the branches in water to make a mild laxative.

OTHER NAMES

RED TWINBERRY • ROCKY MOUNTAIN HONEYSUCKLE

46

1 to 4 inches

April to August

Prefers moist to wet soil, by streams and springs, often in the shade.

DID YOU KNOW?
The common garden pansy is also a species of Viola. *The flowers are rich in vitamins A and C and may be added to salads for flavor and color. The leaves contain soaplike substances, however, and eating too many may cause vomiting.*

Violet (Blue)

Viola adunca
VIOLET FAMILY

A tiny plant with leafy stems $\frac{1}{2}$ to 2 inches long, blue violet usually grows in low clumps.

The flower is blue to deep purple with 5 petals. The lower 3 petals have a white beard marked by dark purple lines. The 2 upper petals bend backward.

The alternate leaves of the blue violet are egg- or heart-shaped, with rounded teeth on the edges.

The Blackfeet Indians applied an infusion of the roots and leaves to sore and swollen joints.

OTHER NAMES
EARLY BLUE VIOLET • WESTERN DOG VIOLET

48

up to 6½ feet

May to July

Prefers moist to dry, open sites in woody to rocky areas, from foothills to mountain forests.

DID YOU KNOW?
The feathery seed floss makes excellent tinder for starting fires.

Western Blue Virgin's Bower

Clematis occidentalis

BUTTERCUP FAMILY

Western Blue Virgin's Bower is a trailing woody vine that climbs by clinging to shrubs and small trees.

The 4 lance-shaped, pale blue to purple sepals look like petals, but these blossoms don't have any petals.

The leaves are opposite and compound, with 3 lance-shaped leaflets. The edges can be toothless to sharply toothed.

Some American Indians used a poultice of Western Blue Virgin's Bower to reduce swelling, and for joint pain.

OTHER NAMES

BLUE CLEMATIS • PURPLE CLEMATIS

1 to 4 feet

June to August

Prefers well-drained soils in open woods and clearings and on mountain slopes.

DID YOU KNOW?
Meriwether Lewis collected beargrass on June 15, 1806, in present-day Idaho and often wrote about the plant in his journals.

Xerophyllum tenax

Beargrass

LILY FAMILY

When in bloom, beargrass has a big, round cluster of small white flowers on a tall stalk surrounded by a clump of long grasslike leaves.

Each tiny, creamy white, star-shaped flower has 6 petals and 6 stamens. The flowers are clustered at the top of the long stem. Most plants only bloom once every 3 to 10 years.

The tough, wiry leaves grow mainly from the base of the plant in large clumps. A few shorter leaves alternate along the stalk.

Meriwether Lewis noted that some Native American tribes dyed the leaves of beargrass and used them to weave colorful baskets.

OTHER NAMES

INDIAN BASKET GRASS • ELK GRASS

4 to 10 inches

March to June

Prefers moist soils in forests and grassy prairies.

DID YOU KNOW?

Meriwether Lewis collected yellow bell in present-day Idaho on May 8, 1806.

Yellow Bell

Fritillaria pudica

LILY FAMILY

Yellow bell usually has a single golden flower that hangs downward like a bell from a bent stalk.

The small golden yellow flower has 3 petals and 3 petal-like sepals. Most plants have a single flower, but occasionally specimens are seen with 2 or 3.

The slender leaves usually occur in a pair and sometimes in a trio.

Meriwether Lewis wrote in his journals, "The bulb is the shape of a biscuit which the natives eat."

OTHER NAMES

YELLOW FRITILLARY • MISSION BELL

1 to 2 feet

June to August

Found in high mountain areas, from forests and moist meadows to rocky slopes and open grasslands.

DID YOU KNOW?
Meriwether Lewis collected this plant in 1806 along the Blackfoot River in present-day Montana.

Zigadenus elegans
Mountain Death Camas
LILY FAMILY

Mountain death camas has a slender stem and long, narrow leaves with parallel veins.

White clusters of flowers are produced at the top of the stem. The 3 creamy white petals and 3 similar sepals form a starlike blossom and have a green heart-shaped gland at their base. Each flower is $\frac{1}{2}$ to $\frac{3}{4}$ inch wide and has 6 stamens and 3 styles.

The grasslike leaves are 4 to 10 inches long and grow mainly from the base of the plant. There are also a few small stem leaves.

If eaten, this poisonous plant may sicken or even kill humans and animals. Because of this, some Indian tribes placed mountain death camas around the perimeter of their encampments to ward off evil spirits.

OTHER NAMES

SHOWY DEATH CAMAS • WHITE CAMAS

FLOWER ACTIVITIES

Note to teachers and parents: The following activities provide opportunities for children to observe, experiment, and engage in hands-on learning. The projects also encourage children to ask questions, which often leads to further investigation. To reinforce learning, these activities are connected to other curriculum areas.

CREATIVE WRITING

Wildflower Poetry

MATERIALS: Photos of various wildflowers.

QUESTION: Why are flowers so appealing to humans?

ACTIVITY: Choose a photo of a wildflower. Write a cinquain (a poem with five lines) describing the flower. As a challenge, try to also use alliteration (where each word starts with the same sound).

CINQUAIN EXAMPLE

1st line	topic	Glacier lily
2nd line	2 words describing line 1	Graceful, gorgeous
3rd line	3 action words ending in "ing"	Glowing, glimmering, glittering
4th line	4 words about the topic	Glistening in the morning dew
5th line	1 word that sums it up	Glorious

TECHNOLOGY

Project BudBurst

MATERIALS: Data collection forms, plant identification cards, and magnifying glasses.

QUESTION: What do scientists do?

ACTIVITY: Join citizens all over the United States collecting plant life cycle data and contributing to an ongoing scientific research project. Simply register with Project BudBurst on the website www.neoninc.org/budburst. Download collection forms and plant identification cards. Observe and collect data about plants at different stages of their life cycle: budding, first bloom, full bloom, and fruit ripening.

VISUAL ARTS

Pounding-out-the-Pigment Quilt Squares

MATERIALS: Hammers or mallets, squares of white cotton cloth, paper, clothes iron, and an assortment of flowers and leaves in different sizes, shapes, and colors. (Often flower shops are willing to donate flowers that are beyond their prime.) Flowers such as geraniums, roses, petunias, and dandelions work well.

QUESTIONS: What is the purpose of flower pigments? Why are flowers different colors? Do certain flower colors or pigments help attract pollinators to the flower?

ACTIVITY: Place a white cotton cloth square on a cutting board or on the floor. Arrange selected flower petals and leaves on the cloth square. If the flower is layered, take it apart and do a few petals at a time. Carefully place a piece of paper over the petals and leaves. Hammer the paper, then lift the paper and peel off the petals and leaves. Use a dry iron on a low temperature to set the pigment. The poundings cannot be immersed in water but can be dry-cleaned. If you want to make the squares into a quilt, add a border and quilt as desired.

SCIENTIFIC WRITING

Germination

MATERIALS: Ziplock bag, three dried lima beans soaked overnight, wet paper towel, string, ruler, and science journal.

QUESTIONS: What are the stages of germination? What happens to the seed coat as the seed sprouts? Which part of the plant grows first?

ACTIVITY: Place the wet paper towel and lima beans in the ziplock bag. Put the sealed bag in a dark spot such as a closet or desk drawer. Record what has happened so far and note observations each day in the science journal. When the first sign of green appears, tape the bag to a window where there is plenty of sun. Check to make sure the paper towel stays moist. As roots and sprouts grow, measure the growth each day with string and rulers. The pieces of string can be glued to the pages of the science journal to record growth. Note when the first leaf appears.

ILLUSTRATED PLANT GLOSSARY

FLOWERS

A flower's job is to make seeds so new plants can grow. Even though there are many different kinds of flowers, they all have some of the same basic parts.

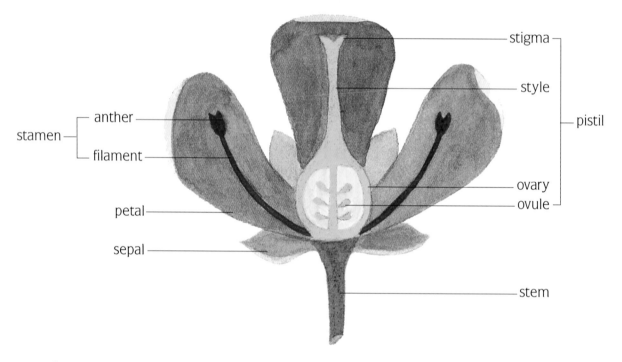

Petals are a special kind of leaf. They surround the center of the flower and are often the most brightly colored part of a flower. **Sepals** are small leaves under a flower. They are usually green, but sometimes they are brightly colored like petals.

In the center of the flower is the **pistil**, the female organ that produces seeds. The **stamen** is the male organ. It consists of a **filament** that supports an **anther**. Inside the anther are powdery yellow grains of **pollen**.

At the top of the pistil is the **stigma**. In a process known as pollination, the stigma collects pollen, which travels down a tube called the **style** to the **ovary**. There it unites with an **ovule** and forms a seed.

The bright colors and sweet scents of flowers attract creatures such as bees, butterflies, and hummingbirds, which fly from flower to flower collecting nectar. As insects and birds visit flowers, grains of pollen may cling to them and be carried to other flowers. The flower helps the pollinator by providing food, while the pollinator helps the flowering plant make seeds.

LEAVES

LEAF ARRANGEMENTS

alternate

opposite

whorled

LEAF SHAPES

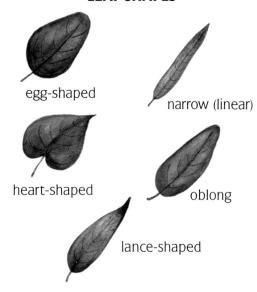

egg-shaped

narrow (linear)

heart-shaped

oblong

lance-shaped

COMPOUND LEAVES
(divided into leaflets)

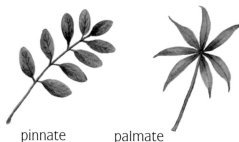

pinnate

palmate

LEAF EDGES

toothed

lobed

smooth

OTHER PLANT TERMS

bract. A modified leaf, often located beneath the petals. In some plants, such as Indian paintbrush, bracts can be so brightly colored that they look like petals.

bulb. A swollen underground food-storing stem.

coniferous. A type of forest with many trees, such as pine, spruce, fir, and cedar, that produce cones.

corm. An underground bulblike enlargement of the stem.

fruit. The seed-bearing part of the plant that develops from a flower.

germinate. When a seed begins to sprout; to start developing or growing.

nectar. A sweet liquid produced by flowers that attracts insects.

stem. The stalk, or support structure, of a flower.

RESOURCES

GUIDE BOOKS

Hunt, Jeff. *Montana Native Plants and Early Peoples*. Helena, MT: Montana Historical Society, 1976.

Kershaw, Linda, Andy MacKinnon, and Jim Pojar. *Plants of the Rocky Mountains*. Edmonton, Alberta: Lone Pine, 1998.

Kimball, Shannon Fitzpatrick, and Peter Lesica. *Wildflowers of Glacier National Park and Surrounding Areas*. Kalispell, MT: Trillium Press, 2005.

Moerman, Daniel E. *Native American Ethnobotany*. Portland, OR: Timber Press, 1998.

Phillips, H. Wayne. *Northern Rocky Mountain Wildflowers*. Helena, MT: Falcon, 2001.

Schiemann, Donald Anthony. *Wildflowers of Montana*. Missoula, MT: Mountain Press, 2005.

Shaw, Richard J., and Danny On. *Plants of Waterton-Glacier National Parks and the Northern Rockies*. Missoula, MT: Mountain Press, 1979.

Snell, Alma Hogan. *A Taste of Heritage*. Lincoln, NE: University of Nebraska Press, 2006.

Stickler, Dee. *Alpine Wildflowers*. Columbia Falls, MT: The Flower Press, 1990.

Stickler, Dee. *Forest Wildflowers*. Columbia Falls, MT: The Flower Press, 1988.

Tilford, Gregory L. *Edible and Medicinal Plants of the West*. Missoula, MT: Mountain Press, 1997.

CHILDREN'S BOOKS

Burns, Diane L. *Wildflowers, Blooms, and Blossoms*. Minnetonka, MN: Northword Press, 1998.

Magley, Beverly. *Montana Wildflowers: A Beginner's Field Guide to the State's Most Common Flowers*. Guilford, CT: Globe Pequot Press, 1993.

WEBSITES

www.americanvioletsociety.org
Information about hundreds of violets around the world.

www.cwnp.org
Over 400 species of native plants in the heart of Washington state.

www.fs.fed.us/wildflowers/kids
Information about wildflowers in our national forests, including coloring books for children.

www.lewisandclarktrail.com
History of the Lewis and Clark expedition with journal excerpts describing plants.

www.montana.plant-life.org
Website with information about wildflowers and other plants in Montana.

www.mountainnature.com
Includes a comprehensive field guide of plants in the Rockies.

www.mtnativeplants.org
Montana Native Plant Society's website.

www.plants.usda.gov
U.S. Department of Agriculture database of plants.

www.swcoloradowildflowers.com
Southwest Colorado's wildflowers, ferns, and trees.

www.wildflowerinformation.org
Wildflower photos, gardening tips, and flower folklore.

www.wildflowers-and-weeds.com
Wildflower identification with helpful illustrations.

www.yellowstonenationalpark.com
Links to information on wildflowers in Yellowstone Park.

ABOUT THE AUTHOR

Sharon Lamar is an educator whose career has spanned more than three decades. She has taught students at every grade level from preschool to college. She has a special interest in enriching elementary science education through outdoor investigations. She is particularly interested in allowing children to connect with nature and become junior naturalists. With her guidance, her students recently designed a pamphlet with illustrations and descriptions of native plants along the Bigfork School District's campus trail.

Sharon is also an illustrator. Her watercolor paintings have been displayed at local juried art shows. Her wildflower illustrations capture the fragile beauty and true essence of the natural world. She and her husband, Steve, also a writer, make their home in Swan Valley, Montana.